D0898008

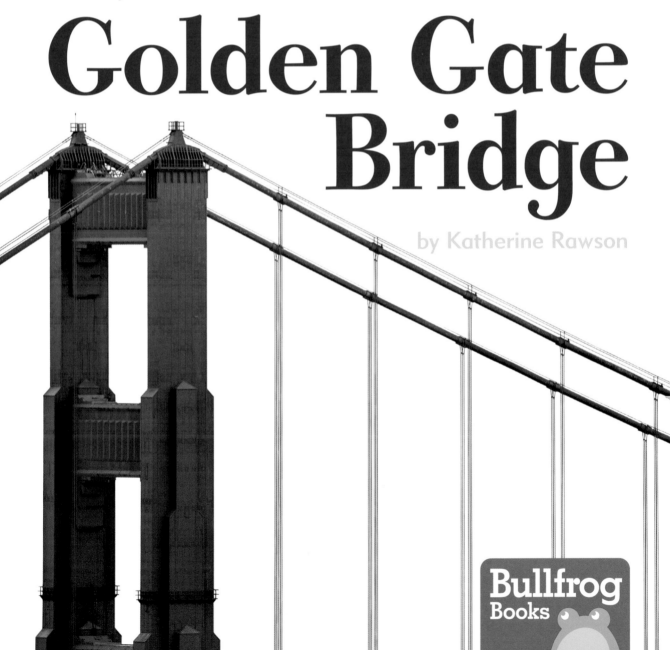

Hello, America!

Golden Gate Bridge

by Katherine Rawson

Bullfrog Books

Ideas for Parents and Teachers

Bullfrog Books let children practice reading informational text at the earliest reading levels. Repetition, familiar words, and photo labels support early readers.

Before Reading

- Discuss the cover photo. What does it tell them?

- Look at the picture glossary together. Read and discuss the words.

Read the Book

- "Walk" through the book and look at the photos. Let the child ask questions. Point out the photo labels.

- Read the book to the child, or have him or her read independently.

After Reading

- Prompt the child to think more. Ask: What's the longest bridge you've ever visited? How big was it?

Bullfrog Books are published by Jump!
5357 Penn Avenue South
Minneapolis, MN 55419
www.jumplibrary.com

Library of Congress Cataloging in Publication Data
Names: Rawson, Katherine, author.
Title: Golden Gate Bridge / by Katherine Rawson.
Description: Minneapolis, Minnesota: Jump!, Inc., 2017.
Series: Hello, America!
"Bullfrog Books." | Includes index.
Identifiers: LCCN 2017032854 (print)
LCCN 2017027398 (ebook)
ISBN 9781624966590 (e-book)
ISBN 9781620318669 (hard cover: alk. paper)
Subjects: LCSH: Golden Gate Bridge
(San Francisco, Calif.)—Juvenile literature.
Golden Gate Bridge (San Francisco, Calif.)
History—Juvenile literature.
Suspension bridges—California—San Francisco
Design and construction—History—Juvenile
literature. | San Francisco (Calif.)—Buildings,
structures, etc.—Juvenile literature.
Classification: LCC TG25.S225 (print)
LCC TG25.S225 R39 2017 (ebook) | DDC 624.2/30979461—dc23
LC record available at https://lccn.loc.gov/2017032854

Editor: Kirsten Chang
Book Designer: Molly Ballanger
Photo Researcher: Molly Ballanger

Photo Credits: Tinnaporn Sathapornnanont/ Shutterstock, cover; Spondylolithesis/iStock, 1; Found Image Holdings Inc/Getty, 3; Oomka/ Shutterstock, 4; Rudy Balasko/Shutterstock, 5; holbox/Shutterstock, 6–7; cdrin/Shutterstock, 8–9; nito/Shutterstock, 10; Underwood Archives/Getty, 11; ullstein bild/Getty, 12–13; kropic1/Shutterstock, 14–15; Otto Greule Jr/Stringer/Getty, 16–17; Travel Stock/Shutterstock, 18; Robert Huberman/ Alamy, 19; Keneva Photography/Shutterstock, 20–21; Luciano Mortula - LGM/Shutterstock, 22; FERNANDO BLANCO CALZADA/Shutterstock, 23tl; Mpanchenko/Shutterstock, 24.

Printed in the United States of America at Corporate Graphics in North Mankato, Minnesota.

Table of Contents

A Long Bridge

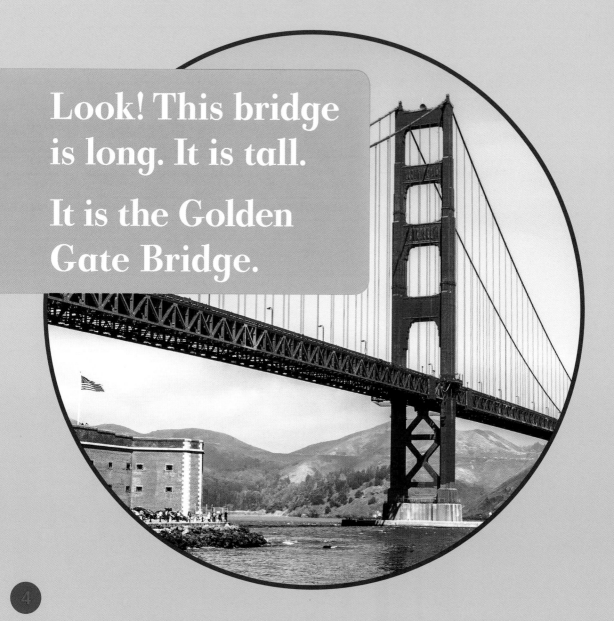

Look! This bridge is long. It is tall.

It is the Golden Gate Bridge.

Golden
Gate
Bridge

Where is it?

San Francisco.

San
Francisco

5

It is a famous landmark.
See its bright color?
It stands out.

People thought a bridge
could not be built here.

The water was too deep.

The waves were
too strong.

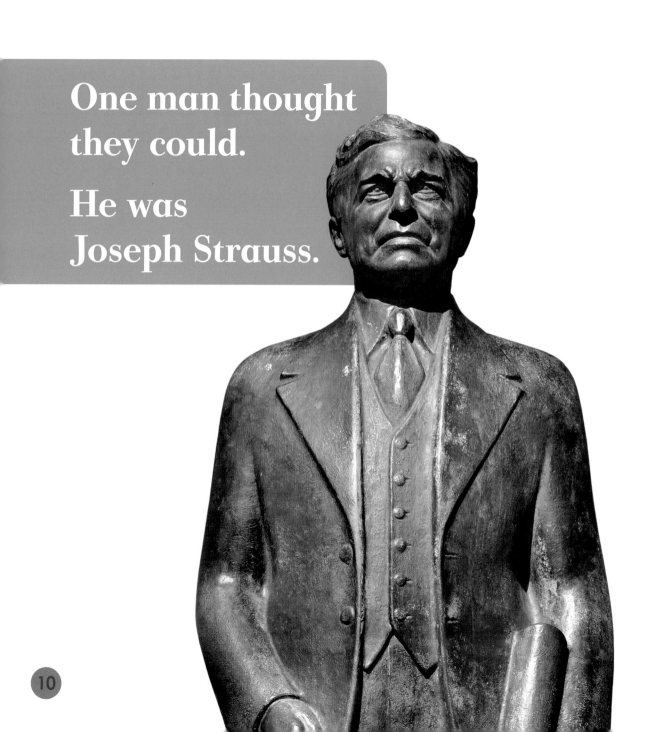

One man thought they could.

He was Joseph Strauss.

He designed it.

11

It opened in 1937.

It was the longest bridge
of its kind in the world.

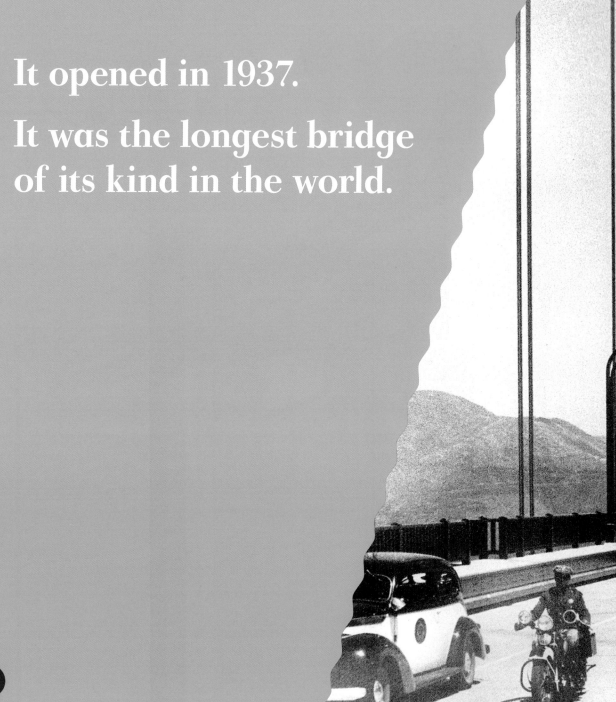

It is more than a mile (1.6 kilometers) long.

It is strong.

It has survived
big earthquakes!

You can drive across it.

You can bike.
You can walk.

The bridge stands tall!

Over the Water

San Francisco

tower

roadway

Golden Gate Strait

Picture Glossary

designed
Drew a plan for.

landmark
An important building, monument, or structure.

earthquakes
Sudden shakings of Earth's surface that often cause damage.

San Francisco
A big city in the state of California.

Index

To Learn More

Learning more is as easy as 1, 2, 3.

1) Go to www.factsurfer.com

2) Enter "GoldenGateBridge" into the search box.

3) Click the "Surf" button to see a list of websites.

With factsurfer.com, finding more information is just a click away.